IT ALL STARTED IN AFRICA

By Suzanne Bowman Williams
Illustrated by Evelynn Jeanette

LUCIDBOOKS

Thanks to the websites below for making their contributions to the Glossary.

Tightrope walker image - dreamstime.com/Pavle Matic
Fishing image - publicdomainvectors.org/Openclipart.org
Hand sign image - shutterstock.com/phipatbig
Ruffled map image - publicdomainvectors.org/Openclipart.org
Slave auction image - publicdomainvectors.org/Openclipart.org
Man running image - publicdomainvectors.org/Openclipart.org
Free state image - Suzanne Bowman Williams
Breaking chains image - dreamstime.com/Andrii Zorii
Ursa Major and Ursa Minor constellations image - shutterstock.com/Mara Fribus
North Star description (revised) - National Park Service/NPS.gov

It All Started in Africa
Copyright © 2020 by Suzanne Bowman Williams
Illustrated by Evelynn Jeanette

Published by Lucid Books in Houston, TX
www.LucidBooksPublishing.com

Hardback ISBN: 978-1-63296-421-2
Paperback ISBN: 978-1-63296-420-5
eBook ISBN: 978-1-63296-422-9

Special Sales: Most Lucid Books titles are available in special quantity discounts. Custom imprinting or excerpting can also be done to fit special needs. Contact Lucid Books at Info@LucidBooksPublishing.com.

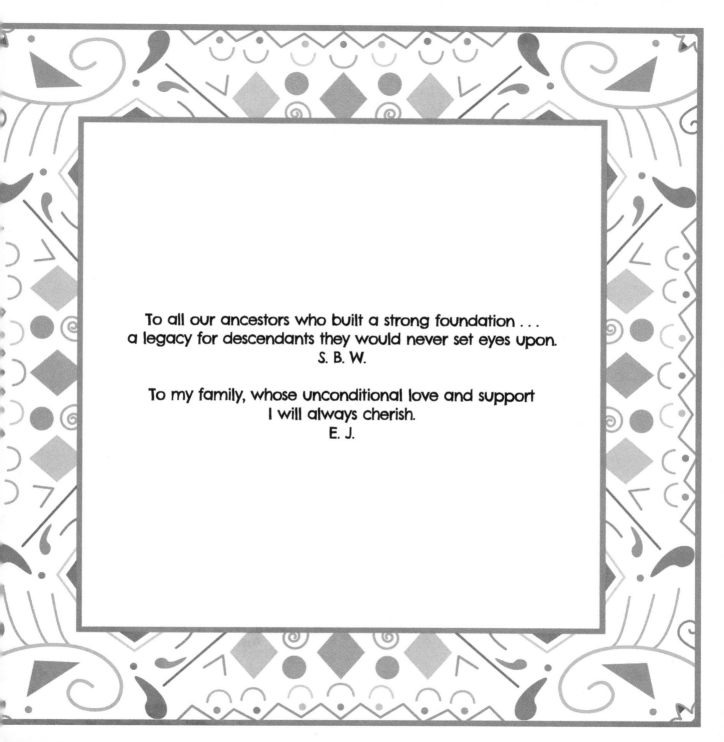

To all our ancestors who built a strong foundation . . .
a legacy for descendants they would never set eyes upon.
S. B. W.

To my family, whose unconditional love and support
I will always cherish.
E. J.

By the sea with her students, one misty day,
A teacher began a story to say,
"We'll journey afar, a long, distant way,

AND IT ALL STARTED IN AFRICA."

The excited children clamored to know
Where this journey would take them and where they would go
"You will learn," smiled the teacher, her eyes aglow,

"AND IT ALL STARTED IN AFRICA."

"In the ancient African lands, we're told
Of marvelous treasures, salt, ivory, and gold

Where in villages, cities, and kingdoms we view
Great rulers, brave warriors, and wise scholars, too.

Where artists used leather, wood, metal, and clay,
They'd hunt, farm, and weave in those times far away.

They'd celebrate life in dance, music, and song
Drums heart-beating, 'Yes! To this land we belong!'

AND IT ALL STARTED IN AFRICA."

"These are the people, strong and bold;
They lived and worked in their sweet village homes,
People with families to love and to hold,

AND IT ALL STARTED IN AFRICA."

"These are the ships that captured and sold
The people away from their sweet village homes
And enslaved those people, strong and bold,

AND IT ALL STARTED IN AFRICA."

"These, the descendants of people enslaved,
Worked for masters to their graves.

Descendants of people captured and sold,
Stolen away from their sweet village homes,
Descendants of people, strong and bold,

AND IT ALL STARTED IN AFRICA."

"The people suffered on, I fear,
Day after day, year after year.

These, the descendants of people enslaved,
Worked for masters to their graves.

Descendants of people captured and sold,
Stolen away from their sweet village homes,
Descendants of people, strong and bold,

AND IT ALL STARTED IN AFRICA."

"One day, Henry and Sallie longed to be free,
To marry, to work, to claim liberty!

They, the descendants of people enslaved,
Who worked for masters to their graves.

Descendants of people captured and sold,
Stolen away from their sweet village homes,
Descendants of people, strong and bold,

AND IT ALL STARTED IN AFRICA."

"This is the North Star burning bright,
It led Henry and Sallie to freedom one night.
The great North Star guiding their dangerous flight,
The North Star of hope for freedom's right.

They, the descendants of people enslaved,
Who worked for masters to their graves.

Descendants of people captured and sold,
Stolen away from their sweet village homes,
Descendants of people, strong and bold,

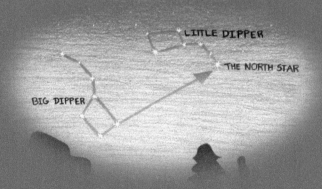

AND IT ALL STARTED IN AFRICA."

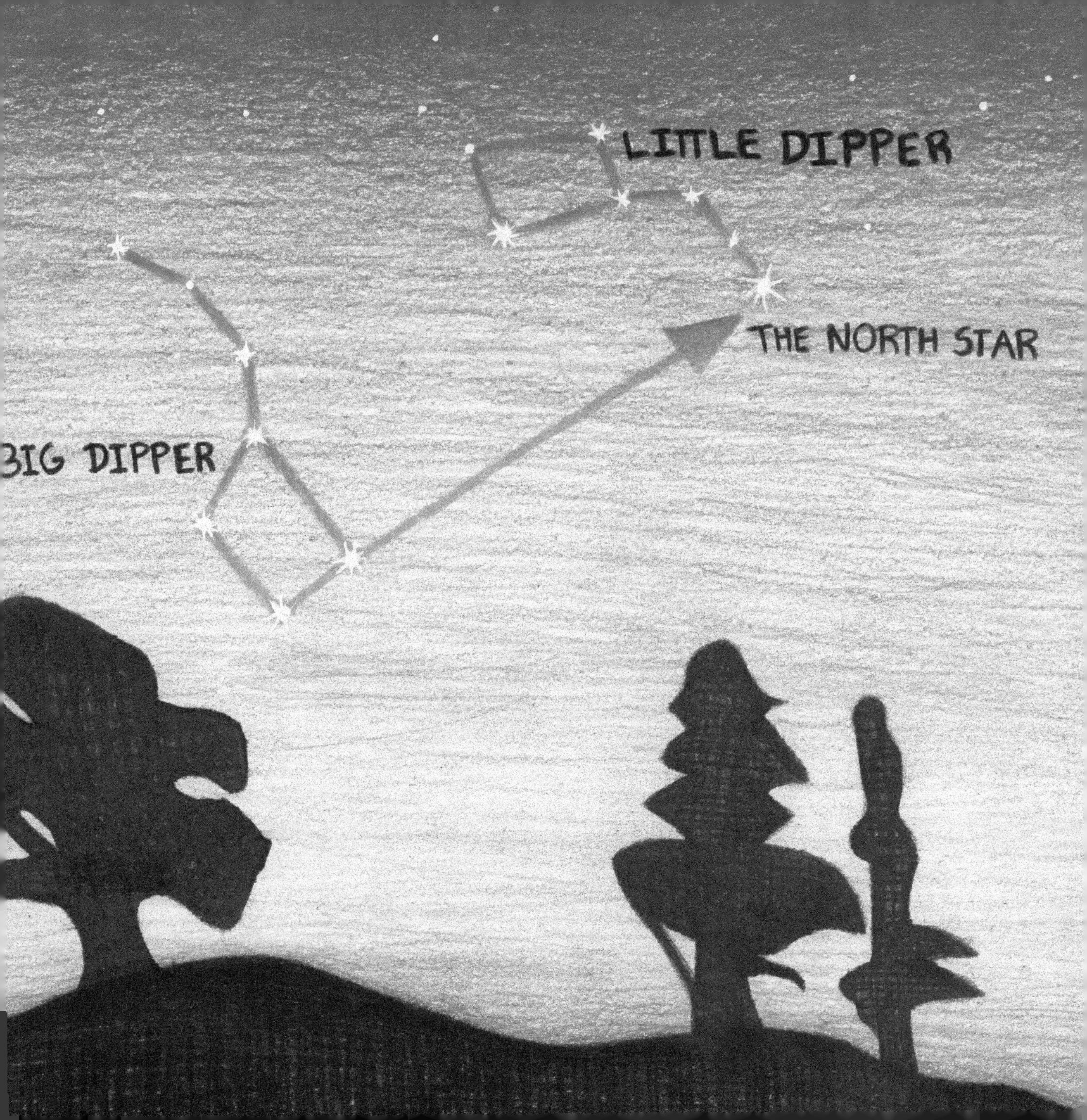
LITTLE DIPPER
THE NORTH STAR
BIG DIPPER

"This is Ohio, a free state, folks said,
Where Henry and Sallie's escape trail led.

They began to live in liberty's light,
To work for a promising future bright.

They, the descendants of people enslaved,
Who worked for masters to their graves.

Descendants of people captured and sold,
Stolen away from their sweet village homes,
Descendants of people, strong and bold,

AND IT ALL STARTED IN AFRICA."

OHIO

"This document President Lincoln signed,
For the ending of slavery it was designed.
Now Henry and Sallie felt truly free
To finally start a family.

To fully live in liberty's light,
Free to claim a future bright!

They, the descendants of people enslaved,
Who worked for masters to their graves.

Descendants of people captured and sold,
Stolen away from their sweet village homes,
Descendants of people, strong and bold,

AND IT ALL STARTED IN AFRICA."

By the President of the United States:

A Proclamation.

Whereas, on the twenty-second day of September, in the year of our Lord one thousand eight hundred and sixty-two, a proclamation was issued by the President of the United States, containing, among other things, the following, to wit:

"That on the first day of January, in the "year of our

"This is Anna, a daughter, born free,
To Henry and Sallie who claimed liberty.

Anna married, started her own family,
In a time of great possibility.

She, a descendant of people enslaved,
Who worked for masters to their graves.

Descendant of people captured and sold,
Stolen away from their sweet village homes,
Descendant of people, strong and bold,

AND IT ALL STARTED IN AFRICA."

"This is Anna's son Roger, a preacher to be,
Who married and chose to live by the sea.

Yes, his mother was Anna, who was born free,
To Henry and Sallie who claimed liberty.

He, a descendant of people enslaved,
Who worked for masters to their graves.

Descendant of people captured and sold,
Stolen away from their sweet village homes,
Descendant of people, strong and bold,

AND IT ALL STARTED IN AFRICA."

"Roger's daughter grew up living by the sea.
He taught her about their family.

From a struggle-filled journey through history,
They'd arrived with a strong, lasting legacy.

She, a descendant of people enslaved,
Who worked for masters to their graves.

Descendant of people captured and sold,
Stolen away from their sweet village homes,
Descendant of people, strong and bold,

AND IT ALL STARTED IN AFRICA."

"And here am I living by the sea,
Telling you children the story of **ME**!

My father was Roger, the preacher to be.
My grandma was Anna, who was born free
To Henry and Sallie who claimed liberty.

I, a descendant of people enslaved,
Who worked for masters to their graves.

Descendant of people captured and sold,
Stolen away from their sweet village homes.
We are the people, strong and bold,

AND IT ALL STARTED IN AFRICA."

Through the mist the sun began to beam
And shone upon the sparkling sea.

A knowing light dawned in the children's wide eyes,
As their destination was realized.

The teacher declared, "Now you children can see.
Now you know that **this** journey leads to **me**!

As they raced home, the children could scarcely believe that

IT ALL STARTED IN AFRICA!

DISCUSSION QUESTIONS

Did the end of this story surprise you?

What important and dangerous choice did Henry and Sallie make?

Why was the North Star so important to Henry and Sallie?

Is there a guiding person in your life who has been a North Star for you?

Can you be a North Star for someone younger than you? How?

Would you like your descendants to remember you for making good choices?

What good choices will you make today to make life better for yourself and for others?

GLOSSARY

The vocabulary definitions in this glossary are focused
mainly on their meanings according to this story.

BOLD  Willing to meet danger or take risks.

CAPTURE  The act of catching or gaining control by force or trickery.

CLAIM  To take something as one's own; something that one has a right to have.

DESCENDANT 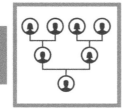 A child of great-grandparents and all ancestors who lived years before.

DESTINATION  The place to which a person is going.

DOCUMENT  A written or printed paper that gives factual (true) information about or proof of something; for example, a driver's license.

ENSLAVE  To force people to give up their freedom and spend their lives obeying and working for their owners, also called masters; being treated as property that could be bought and sold.

FLIGHT  The act of running away from a dangerous or unpleasant situation or place.

FREE STATE  A state of the United States in which slavery was prohibited (not allowed) before the Civil War.

JOURNEY

An act of traveling from one place to another taking many days (like a road trip) or many years (like a life journey).

LEGACY

Anything that is passed down from ancestor or someone who came before, such as money, property, life attitudes, memories, opportunity.

LIBERTY

Freedom from being limited or controlled; the right to free choices and actions.

NORTH STAR

Little Dipper
(Little Bear or Ursa Minor)

North Star
(Polaris)

Big Dipper
(Big Bear or Ursa Major)

The brightest star in the group of st called the Little Dipper, or Ursa Mi (Latin for "Little Bear"); Polaris or Pole S which points to the north.

The **North Star** played a key role in help enslaved people find their way—a beac to true north and freedom. Escap **enslaved** people could find it by locat the Big Dipper, a well-recognized gro of stars most visible in the night sky in winter and spring.

Finding the **North Star** means you kn the direction north.

It is the author's opinion that a person can be a **North Star**, too—someone you c count on and who is always there to guide you in the right direction.

AUTHOR'S NOTE

Henry and Sallie Beard (seated) pictured here with eight of their sixteen children (circa 1925)

one of Southern California's typical misty coastal mornings, as Black History Month approached, I was looking a book to share with my fifth grade students. It had to be a book that would encompass the African American erience from ancient Africa to recent times; a book that would give them an overview of African American ory. As I searched several libraries, I found many great books on various facets of Black history, but none that sented its scope over thousands of years.

r to this search, while visiting my family in Oberlin, Ohio, I received a photograph of my Grandma Anna's ily (above). I learned more about her parents, my great-grandparents Henry and Sallie, who had escaped r enslavement in Kentucky. I was awed by the courage it took for them to risk running away from bondage.

this in mind, I decided to create a "copy, cut, and paste" big book for my students. It would chronicle African erican history interlaced with my family's journey leading to me, their teacher. My class was quite surprised at closing revelation!

er, after moving to a second grade assignment, I crafted the story in this book. It is a shorter, lyrical version of original big book, presented in rhyme, rhythm, and repetition. These three tools not only promote beginning acy but also engage and motivate young and older audiences alike.

ACKNOWLEDGMENTS

I would like to express my gratitude to
the following individuals:

To God who is my continually guiding North Star.

To my parents, Roger and Marlene Bowman, who have exemplified our strong, lasting family legacy. It is my privilege to pass this gift on to my remarkable children, their children, and my descendants to come, though I may never set eyes upon them.

I am gladly in the debt of my gifted illustrator-granddaughter, Evelynn, and her dedication to accomplishing our project. I was sorry to see it come to a close, but I have a feeling that this won't be our last collaboration!

To all the elementary school principals and teachers who offered me opportunities to present this story to their students.

To the Write On writers' group, led by author, Jaine Toth. Their talents were instrumental in the fine-tuning of this work.

Last, but far from least, I'm extremely grateful for my amazing husband, DeGolden; the faithful sounding board and patient encourager in spite of my over-analytical ways. You deserve some extra-good fishing days!

Printed in the USA
CPSIA information can be obtained
at www.ICGtesting.com
LVHW070034300324
775867LV00005B/46